FROM THE FOUR–CHAMBERED HEART:
In Tribute to Anaïs Nin

edited by Marie Lecrivain

SYBARITIC

PRESS

Published by
Sybaritic Press
12530 Culver Blvd.
Suite 3
Los Angeles, CA 90066
www.sybpress.com

ISBN: 9781-4675-8136-3
Cover photo - Aunia Kahn
Printed in the United States of America
First Edition
July 2013

Table of Contents

Introduction

Anaïs Nin is not for the faint of heart. She wore many hats; model, world traveler, diarist (possibly the world's most renowned), a writer's writer, literary critic, wife, actress, teacher, muse, and, patron of the arts. She was also a pathological liar (as witnessed in her rearranged/expurgated diaries), a bigamist, a willing participant - as an adult - in incestuous acts, and, possibly... a sociopath.

Reader, if you've not yet cast this volume aside then you're probably someone who's familiar with myriad facets of Nin's personality. You're someone who's learned to appreciate the genius of Nin's work, in spite of, or, in appreciation of the complex person she represented. The genius of Nin's work lay in her willingness to creatively address the parts of herself that most deeply affected her life. Her work paved the way for writers like me, and the contributors to this anthology, to do the same.

From the Four-Chambered Heart: In Tribute to Anaïs Nin, brings together a diverse mixture of writers, poets, and artists whose work has been inspired by the words and the life of Anaïs Nin. **Aunia Kahn**'s gorgeous front cover artwork pays tribute to both Nin's literary and erotic beauty. **Angel Uriel Perales**'s, "Iced Water on the Table," explores the idea of failed intimacy that marked many of Nin's short stories. **Meghan Elison**'s poem "Anaïs," draws parallels between herself and Nin's experiences within the nuances of sexual identity. **Hattie Quinn**'s "Concentrate of the Poetry," playfully and erotically recounts what happens when 'booth babes' and a shared copy of Nin's *Delta of Venus* combine. **Deborah L. Warner**'s essay, "Perspectives Across a Dinner Table," addresses the prejudices that still exist against women writers who dare to write in genres, including erotica, that are still thought of by many to be exclusively male. **Pam Ward**'s poetic narrative, "Anaïs's Husband," describes the aftermath of Nin's death as experienced by Nin's first (and legal) husband, Hugo.

There are many people to thank in the making of this anthology, but, I will keep it to a minimum: first, my oldest and best friend, **Sigrid Hudson Bishop**, who, 20 years ago placed a volume of Nin's *Little Birds* in my hands and strongly encouraged me to broaden my literary horizons; **Barbara Kraft**, the author of *Anaïs Nin: The Last Days, A Memoir*, whose bravery in writing about her relationship with Nin, in part, inspired me put together this anthology; **Deborah L. Warner**, my publishing partner and fellow writer of erotica, for never letting the bastards get her down; **Jon Cunningham**, for his tireless work, artistry, and patience in formatting, as well as crafting this book into being; and, finally, to **Anaïs Nin**, who reminds us that the truth of *who we are* comes out in every word we write - and to never back down from what we create.

Marie C. Lecrivain
July 2013

This book is dedicated to my dear friends, Sigrid Hudson Bishop, *an amazing woman who first introduced me to enigma that is Anaïs, and, to* D.L. Warner, *whose continues to to set the writing bar higher than the sky.*

Sandy Anderson has been published in *Weber Studies, Eclectica, Stickman Review, Sugarhouse Review, Harpur Palate, Forge,* and *Ellipsis.* Ghost Planet Press published her book *At the Edge in White Robes* in 1978, and her chapbook, *Jeanne Was Once a Player of Pianos,* is available through Limberlost Press. Her poetry is included in the anthologies *New Poets of the American West,* edited by Lowell Jaeger, and *Great and Peculiar Beauty* edited by Terry Tempest Williams and Thomas Lyon. Her awards include the Salt Lake City Mayor's Award in Literature in 1997, the Writers at Work Writing Advocate Award in 1995, and a listing as one of the *Catalyst Magazine 100* in 2013. She has been involved in the literary community since the 1960s, and is the founder of City Art: the longest-running reading series in Utah. She has been artist in residence at several local high schools and given workshops to many different groups, including veterans and the disabled. She recently edited and published her fourth anthology of work by those with disabilities. She lives in Salt Lake City with her husband, two dogs and six guinea pigs.

Kissing Anaïs Nin Goodbye

after Gerald Stern

Every city has monuments that rise
               like a past
                              we glorify
but the Coliseum has lost
               its lions,
       Kom Ombro pools are empty
                       of crocodiles,
and the Taj Mahal never contained
               two lovers,
                              only the memory.

Moroni still flies over
                       my city,
               but it's a bronzed
                              flight,
still, not unlike the details
               omitted from your published journals.

You were a blueprint
                       for balance,
       a West Coast husband
                       and an East Coast,
       a houseboat on the Seine
               and a New York apartment.

You paved the roads
                       with silk scarves,
       the bodies
                       with beads.

The cities are smokier now,
               but the smoke is not
                       transparent like your party
                                      costume.
It is heavy like an angel
       chipped off
                       a cathedral
       and placed
                       in a museum.

3

Anaïs Nin on the Grand Canyon Rim

The mind has rivers that cut deep.
If I scrunch my eyes hard
the jagged walls soften,
make a pastel collage of themselves.
My father's music floats like a silk scarf
on the surface of the water
that I imagined would be the current
I would drink from,
and the abandoned creek beds
would yield prehistoric fossils
water-polished into jewels.

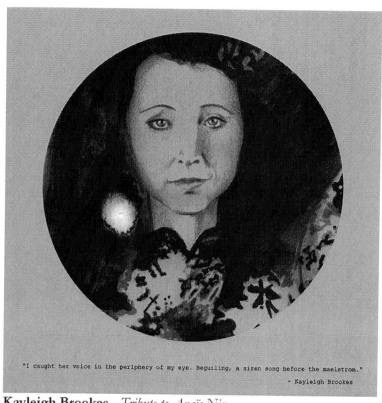

"I caught her voice in the periphery of my eye. Beguiling, a siren song before the maelstrom."

— Kayleigh Brookes

Kayleigh Brookes - *Tribute to Anaïs Nin*

Shawn Aveningo is an award-winning poet who was voted Best Female Poet in 2009 in the SN&R Reader's Poll. Her poetry has appeared in dozens of publications including *Pirene's Fountain*, *Tincture Journal*, *Poetry Now*, *Featherlit*, *Convergence*, *Survivor's Review*, *POETZ*, *Cliterature*, *WTF*, *Savage Melodies & Last Call Serenades*, *The Oddity*, *Wait a Minute, I Have to Take Off My Bra*, and *Seattle Erotic Anthology*. Shawn hosts the "Verse on the Vine" poetry show in Folsom, CA (www.verseonthevine.com) and has been a featured poet in Sacramento, San Francisco, Sausalito, Seattle and St Louis, and hopes to entertain audiences in more cities that start with the letter 'S'. Shawn's a Show-Me girl from Missouri, graduated Summa Cum Laude from University of Maryland and is a very proud mother of three. Shawn is also a founding member of the performing group, Poetica Erotica (www.Poetica-Erotica.com) and owner/partner of The Poetry Box (www.ThePoetryBox.com)

Kayleigh Brookes, of 'The Little Room at House of Brookes," is a graduate of illustration from the University of Central Lancashire, England, who credits a large percentage of her artistic talents to hours spent as a child drawing in "the little room," with her beloved late grandfather, a talented painter, on the beautiful isle of Anglesey.

Kayleigh now has a "little room" to call her own in which she strives to capture the beauty of those people, objects, times and places which inspire her, and to put a little something of herself into them.

Dear Henry

I must warn you my tongue has no governor.
Words whispered as winds howl through naughty pines.
Hush, I hear angel's wings approaching.
My ankles crisscross in the small of your back.
I play your vertebrae, keys to my saxophone blues.
My soulful siren song, "hallelujah."
I shout to a deity whose belief I do not follow.
Heavenly voyeurs, stars just beyond my reach.

Heavenly voyeurs, stars just beyond my reach.
Hush, I hear angel's wings approaching.
My soulful siren song, "hallelujah."
I shout to a deity whose belief I do not follow.
Words whispered as winds howl through naughty pines.
I must warn you my tongue has no governor.
My ankles crisscross in the small of your back.
I play your vertebrae, keys to my saxophone blues.

I play your vertebrae, keys to my saxophone blues.
My ankles crisscross in the small of your back.
Words whispered as winds howl through naughty pines.
I shout to a deity whose belief I do not follow.
My soulful siren song, "hallelujah."
Heavenly voyeurs, stars just beyond my reach.
Hush, I hear angel's wings approaching.
I must warn you my tongue has no governor.

Lynne Bronstein has written four books of poetry, *Astray from Normalcy, Roughage, Thirsty in the Ocean,* and *Border Crossings.* She works as a newspaper reporter the *Culver City Observer,* has written for numerous music magazines and web sites, has published poetry and short fiction in numerous magazines (and web sites), and was winner of the first runner up short fiction prize for *poeticdiversity's* Fiction Contest in 2006. She has received certificates of appreciation from two non-profits for her work mentoring adults and children in writing.

Black Swan

How odd to describe one's love for a person
By recalling the upward sweep of her lashes.
Yet that is what I remember about her.
Black crescents craning up like swan's necks
To glide on the water of her eyes.
Thin-plucked brows above, hovering over
Their charges, ironic duennas.
A quickly-changing picture passes over
The screen of the iris—
A look alert, so wide it opens a door.
A gaze that makes me humble,
Determined to recall her words,
Letters like black swans underlined three times—
Her gift, her love, to me.

(From *Roughage*, © 1977 by Lynne Bronstein)

Deborah Edler Brown is a poet, performer, journalist, teacher and author. She was the 2005 winner of Kalliope's Sue Saniel Elkind Poetry, the 1997 National Head-to-Head Haiku Champion, and a member of the 1998 Los Angeles National Slam Team. As a journalist, Brown was a stringer for *Time* magazine, and she is co-author of *Grandparents as Parents: A Survival Guide to Raising a Second Family* [Guilford Press, 1995]. She was born in Brazil, raised in Pittsburgh, and teaches creative writing in Los Angeles and online. She is in love with the magical properties of words.

Such Stuff as Dreams

Annabelle almost couldn't get any sleep these days for all the talking, the pulling of covers, the opening and shutting of windows. It had begun with the dreams. One night, she was lying down alone, yet again, in her queen-size bed, holding a pillow against her belly for comfort, and then Kirk slipped into her sleep. She hadn't spoken to him in years, but she was happy, in the dream, to see him, to feel his hand on the small of her back, the heat that always seemed to flame in the air between them, even that last day when she watched his back move forward down the driveway, the space between them stretching long and hot like a Texas siesta, until the car turned the corner, and she had to grab a sweater.

When she woke in the morning, there was a smile on her lips, and she realized that she had pushed half her blankets onto the floor. She smiled throughout the day at what dreams can do. She had slept alone, but her body curled softly, as if she had made love.

The next night she dreamed of David. Cool, moody David, whose long fingers had washed lavender through her hair whenever she was stressed or sad. In the dream, he was drawing a rose-filled bath, offering to rub sesame oil into her tired shoulders. There were bedroom sounds in that dream, or sounds in the bedroom – the scraping of a chair, a door closing – but she only realized it later. In the dream, in that moment, she had her legs wrapped around David's thin torso as rose petals tumbled through the water like ruby fish.

Her hair was damp in the morning. "I must have a fever," she thought and took two Advil, even though her skin was cool to the touch.

"Did you know you keep traces of everyone you've ever slept with?"asked Gina over lunch.

"Hmmm?" said Annabel. She was lost in the frosty cream of her Mint Mochachino.

"It's energy," said Gina. "Like photo bleed, ghost images." She tapped the magazine with a long, pink nail. "This guy says we leave bits of our energy on everyone we sleep with. He recommends aura cleansing or something. I wonder where you do that..."

Annabelle drew one finger along the rim of her plastic cup and bit her lower lip. How many guys had she slept with? She tried to count. It all seemed so long ago. Her aura was probably an empty train station by now.

Jacob appeared that night. Jacob, wearing only a chef's hat and apron, pressing his hands into white, soft dough, making croissants in all kinds of un-crescent shapes, shapes she could never have brought to the office had this not been a dream. Somewhere she heard water running, but Jacob was pressing a warm roll against her stomach and whispering creative uses for jam.

The flour in the hallway was the first real warning. She had not baked in months, and yet there it was, two days after the girl had been in to clean. The bright spring day had no impact on her. In fact, she almost left her skin when Gina said, "What about that flower!"

"Flour?"

"That long-stemmed rose Mark sent Nancy. I've never seen such a beauty."

Alan was in the living room the moment she closed her eyes that night. She almost couldn't hear what he was trying to say, one hand on the piano key, one on her bare thigh. She thought she heard water running and noises in the bedroom. A smell of baking almost overpowered the Halston that Alan always wore, which he was seriously trying to share with her, skin to skin.

"In a moment," she whispered, curiosity trumping desire, and walked carefully toward the kitchen, with Alan following behind her like a quickly wrapped shawl.

There were several people in the kitchen. Jacob was making donuts. He was shaking powdered sugar on a fresh tray of donut holes and across the breasts of Betsey Mason, the girl he'd dated in high school. Betsey looked at Annabelle in triumph and bit a hole.

Before Annabelle could respond, the bedroom door slammed and Kirk ran past, followed by his ex-wife Susie and her husband Jim. Jim grabbed a donut and headed toward the bathroom, where six naked people clustered in and around her tub: David, Martha, his first girlfriend, Jim, Scott, the man David left her for, and two women she'd never seen.

"Who wants donuts?" called Jacob from the hallway. Alan still had his hand on her shoulder, but the other one grabbed the fresh, hot dough.

"It's time to wake up," she said firmly.

"Hmm?" asked Alan, his mouth full of sugar.

"Pinch me, I need to wake up."

"Ouch!" she yelled. She was clutching her bottom when she woke, holding a spot that would surely bruise, but relieved to be awake.

"You okay?" asked a sleepy male voice. She almost didn't want to look.

"Yeah, keep it down," said a female voice.

"Aw. Now I'm up, too. Someone hand me another donut."

(previously published in *The Smoking Poet*, Fall/Winter 2011-2012)

Hélène Cardona is the author of *Dreaming My Animal Selves* (Salmon Poetry 2013) and *The Astonished Universe* (Red Hen Press 2006). She holds a Master's in American Literature from the Sorbonne, taught at Hamilton College and LMU, and received fellowships from the Goethe Institut and the Universidad Internacional de Andalucía. She translated the Lawrence Bridges film *Muse of Fire* for the NEA, *What We Carry* by Dorianne Laux, and Eloise Klein Healy into French, and the poetry of her father José Manuel Cardona, Rimbaud, Baudelaire, Aloysius Bertrand and Jean-Claude Renard into English. She is also an actor (Chocolat) and dream analyst.

Strength

After the storm
emerald diaphanous waves
envelop golden oceans bled by sun
Ghosts and demons rest
dismantle shields
In radiant light, latent powers awaken
I'll drink your tears, communion
of souls, transcend pain into love
give myself over to the sublime and ferocious
May I fall beyond earth
unbind all energies, the unrevealed
Resting on the mountain's face, kissed
by clouds, taking in the whole sky
your blueness comes through each time
wonderful magic of holding silence
I use geography to find myself
mind and heart in unison
Underneath precise physical laws
and the apparent play of chance
lies mysterious healing power
Let's share exquisite pomegranates
smear them in each other's faces

Diane Dehler studied Creative Writing at San Francisco State University and received the Outstanding Student of the Year Award when she graduated. She have published in several literary journals; most recently in *The Criterion: an international journal in English, Contemporary Literary Horizon* and *The Taj Mahal Review*.

Images of Love

I
I touch you staring into a
fire's crackling flame. We are

Only shadows on the wall
for there is no time.

II
The evening is short;
surrounds us draws us apart,
reunites us.

We are the only music
that is real.

III
When you came to me
I knew at once, Adam. You
were forbidden fruit.

Soft are your firm hands
on me. We have always
known each other.

IV
My fear of you binds me to the
moving postures of this bed.
Is this fear love?

VI
You leap from the music
of, Swan Lake, a prince but

Tonight I am Clytemnestra,
wearing sackcloth and ash. We
do not touch.

VII
We make love by a
seashore. I marvel at your sun

Drenched hair and throw my lace
dress carelessly aside.

VIII
Sand wedges batik designs on
our footsteps. A collector of

Seaweed and tides finds my
dress covered with wet sand &

Takes it home. You love
me without it.

IX
Eroticism is a mirage,
touched it disappears.

Who told you, you could
touch my thigh?

X
When the sailor's red sun
sinks low in the sky.

In that second we will know
all desire.

Venus Retrograde

Private conversation
on a couch of love.
Firm cushions and
a hard wood floor.
White sun – clouds
burst into light. A
buzzing bee hums a
song on the window
ledge. Yet the person
undressed was missing.
Multiple identities fly
by. When they are
coming they are going.
A rhythm that never
stops. People making
love in the mind's eye.

Lori Desrosiers has a book of poems, *The Philosopher's Daughter* (Salmon Poetry) and a chapbook, *Three Vanities* (Pudding House). Her poems have appeared in *New Millenium Review, Contemporary American Voices, BigCityLit, Concise Delights, Blue Fifth Review, Pirene's Fountain, The New Verse News, Common Ground Review,* and many more, including a prompt in *Wingbeats*, a book of writing exercises from Dos Gatos Press. Her MFA in Poetry is from New England College. She is editor and publisher of *Naugatuck River Review*, a journal of narrative poetry.

Anaïs in Paris

A glance slips between thighs.
I know it is my lover's.
His eyes caress, without touch
behind the screen, watching
as the other tugs at my blouse
breaking top button, sweat.
Silk melts under hidden gaze,
blue eyes burn through gauze curtain.
Pale legs shake beneath his chest.
I cry out, careful to name no one.

Meg Elison is a student at UC Berkeley. She writes for *The Daily Californian*.

Anaïs

I tell so many lies I have to write them down
and keep them in the lie box
so I can keep them straight. - **Anaïs Nin**

Truth or dare, dear Anaïs?
Sisters under skin
Your secrets are my secrets
And I know you will never tell

I dare you to kiss a girl.
No? You talk a big game, but you'd never do it
I did it
And she was a fever that would never break
Alright, tell me the truth about your dad
And don't write a poem to hide behind

No?
No truth, no dare.
Just a piece of a map.
I've been collecting,
I got one from Anne Sexton
and another from Erica Jong
I see where this is going.

Time for me to stand on this spot marked X
And tell the truth
And dare.

Writer/photographer **Alexis Rhone Fancher** is a member of Jack Grapes' L.A. Poets & Writers Collective. Her work has been published or is forthcoming in *RATTLE, BoySlut, The Mas Tequila Review, The Poetry Super Highway, The Juice Bar, Cultural Weekly, High Coupe, Gutter Eloquence Magazine, Tell Your True Tale, Bare Hands, Downer Magazine*, the anthology, *Poised In Flight* and elsewhere. Her photographs have been published world-wide. In 2013 she was nominated for a Pushcart Prize. She is poetry editor of *Cultural Weekly*. www.alexisrhonefancher.com

Walk All Over You -

inspired by Anaïs Nin's A Spy In The House of Love

The stiletto boots in the back of my closet are
restless, long to stroll the 3rd Street Promenade,
looking for a red silk bustier. A Louis Vuitton bag.
A lover who won't let me down.

The stiletto boots in the back of my closet
want to party, want to grab my feet,
climb my calves, hug my thighs. They're
ready for action. Ready to put on a skintight
Versace. Ready to head for the club.

They want to clack on terrazzo floors,
totter from great heights, see the world.
Escape the flats, the Mary Jane's, the penny
loafers, the two-toned, two-faced saddle Oxfords
that guard the closet door.

The stiletto boots in the back of my closet
want to walk all over you, punish you for
cheating, make you pay.
They long to wrap themselves around
you, put you in a headlock, rake your thighs -
want to lead you into

Debauchery.
Saran Wrap.
Whipped cream.
Wesson Oil.
Room service.

Remember?

The stiletto boots have a short attention span, choose
not to remember why they were banished, or what you
did. They're desperate to reclaim you,
dig their heels into your shortcomings,
make little marks up and down your libido.
Welcome you home.
My stilettos can't forget you.

My stilettos can't move on.
My stilettos will forgive you.
Even if I cannot.

They bear the scuff marks
of your betrayal far better than do I.

Like the last time and the time before.
They want to get started, head out the door.
Who do you think gave me those fucking boots,
anyway?

Michelle Angelini - *Rose Shadow*

Frank William Finney's poems have appeared in such publications as *Danse Macabre, Paris/Atlantic, Staple Competition Poems,* and *The Green Hills Literary Lantern.* He lives, writes and teaches (at Thammasat University) in Bangkok, Thailand.

Michelle Angelini (aka Rina Rose) has been a SoCal resident for over 33 years. She writes poetry for various San Gabriel Valley publications and calendars and is hooked on animal, nature, and street photography. Michelle graduated from CSUN with a BA in English/Creative Writing. Right now she is blissfully retired until she finds part-time work and makes her home in Hollywood with a cat, Sasha (her editor and critic) and fish, Kai - her roommates. Michelle is currently working on publishing a first book of her poems and photographs.

Anaïs Nin Waves by the Waves

Waves roll their eyes
towards towel gulls of August
veiled eyes savour
charades by the canal
parades of fish-tail
march along the shoreline
trading glance for dance
and sneer for suppressed desire
blue-green laughter echoes
along the sea wall
where Anaïs's smile hovers over
Neptune's myriad tongues
in eternal French kiss

(previously published in *Prophetic Voices: An International Literary Journal*, XXI in 1994; *The Dissolution of the Sparkling Bridge* collection of poems, Suksit Siam, 1998)

John FitzGerald is a poet, writer, editor, and attorney in Los Angeles. A dual citizen of the United States and Ireland, he graduated from the University of West Los Angeles School of Law, where he was editor of the Law Review. His newest work, *The Mind*, was published by Salmon Poetry in 2011. His fourth collection is forthcoming from Salmon Poetry in 2014.

Five

Love is one.
Faith, desire, and truth are others.
Where do we keep them?

Such words could all be given numbers,
as were the numbers names. Pictures too, for that matter.
Matter boils down to rules of a game that no one plays.

The mind could be a very large place indeed,
or it could fit at the end of this sentence,
depending on what we choose to believe.

(From *The Mind* , copyright 2011 Salmon Poetry)

Born in a back alley of Pigalle (in Paris), **M. Justine Gerard** loves short stories, the leaves of lotus flowers, the brush of blue velvet against the backs of her knees, and the novels of Michel Houellebecq. Ms. Gerard has resumed writing after a three-year hiatus. She lives within spitting distance of West L.A., but, still claims Echo Park as her true home.

Anni and the Order of Perfectibilis

"You are the only woman who ever answered the demands of my imagination."
— Anaïs Nin, Henry and June: From "A Journal of Love"—The
Unexpurgated Diary of Anaïs Nin

Anni arrived, breathless, the wind at her back, every strand of
her blond faux-hawk in place. She knocked, per the instructions –
two short raps with her left fist, one palm slap with the right hand,
and then, three fingernail taps with the left. The door opened. A
hand reached out. She tickled the palm of the hand and bent to kiss
the middle finger. Once done, the door opened wide enough to let
her inside.

The foyer was lit by two gilded candelabras embellished with
wax and bad taste. Anni was quickly stripped of her Hot Topic
anarchist wear, but allowed to retain her crotchless fishnets and
original purple Doc Martins she'd inherited from her British punk-
rock aunt. She shivered with anticipation; her milky breasts stood at
attention, nipples at the ready. She suppressed the urge to fondle her
faux-hawk, which she did in times of stress. She kept her hands at
her sides while two other acolytes swept over her body with a pair
of feather dusters and a third measured her head, wrists, and waist
with a protractor.

Once done, the trio escorted Anni down a long dark hall. At
the end of the hall was a door. The first acolyte opened the door;
the second and third pushed her into a small closet. Surprised, she
turned, but was stopped into silence by a quick tweak on her left
nipple. On cue, her vagina started to water. Excited, she squeezed
her legs together.

The door closed behind her. Anni massaged her left breast,
fondled the aroused nipple, and then, remembered that this was not
allowed. Her hands cautiously fumbled until she found the garments
on a hanger. She dressed carefully, taking extra care to make sure
everything was straight, an almost impossible task in total darkness.
Once done, she stood and waited... and waited... and waited... The
garments, with their unfamiliar closures, constricted her. She found
herself standing tall in an effort to keep her waist and back from
spasming. Her breaths became more shallow. Her neck began to
ache.

The door opened. She blinked against the sudden intrusion
of light. Two pairs of hands seized Anni. A blindfold fastened over

her eyes. The hands gently pushed her down onto something velvety and soft. Her body was maneuvered into an odalisque. She tensed as she felt herself being lifted into the air. As she struggled to maintain her precarious balance, she held her breath. The air currents changed from cold to warm once she was lowered to the ground.

Anni lay still. She wondered what would happen next. Up to this point, she'd been carefully instructed not to make a sound, to speak only when spoken to. She heard a small movement beside her, the sound of satin whispered against her slim legs. She felt a cool hand against her face. The fingers, gently insistent, drifted down to her mouth, teased her lips, and then parted them to insert an imperious finger. Immediately, Anni's eager tongue - hungry for contact - sucked on the finger.

"Sisters, we are here tonight to welcome a new initiate among us. Who here among us has been trapped in the dichotomy of what being a woman really means?"

"All of US!"

"And, what must we do to overcome this burden?"

"We must die in perfection!"

The finger withdrew and set itself against Anni's lips.

"Anni, are you willing to die in perfection?" The finger withdrew.

Anni swallowed. This was the moment she'd been waiting for:
"Kill me."

The hand covered her mouth as a pair of soft lips brushed against her forehead.

"As you wish."

She heard movement. Her heart thudded in her chest. Her arms were placed over her head, joined at the wrists and tied tightly together. She felt silken cords dig into her wrists. Anni's legs were held far apart as her skirts were lifted, and her tights were torn from legs. She felt the warmth breath of an unknown mouth against her thighs. Her vagina started to sweat. She tried desperately to lift her hips as the mouth moved closer.

The mouth stopped, inhaled Anni's scent as her legs trembled with erotic tension. She felt a tongue brush against her newly shaved lips and then delve into her wet core. Anni tried not to scream as the tongue worked back and forth inside her, as it brought her to the pitch of exhalation... withdraw... and, began again.

34

The tongue withdrew. Another took its place. The second moved in and out like a piston, drove Annie quickly to the edge, withdrew, and was replaced with a fatter, slower tongue that teased Anni's clitoris until she was ready to scream... yet, still - she remained silent. Her wrists worked desperately against the silken cords, her thighs ached. Tongue after tongue teased, taunted, brought her to the edge, and left her breathless.

The last tongue withdrew. Anni's vagina burned with need. Her chest heaved, but, through it all, she remained silent. The mysterious hand descended on Anni's right thigh, stroked it softly until her tremors subsided.

"My sisters, Anni has passed the first crucial test. She has been brought to the edge of oblivion, and not uttered a sound. She stands on the edge of perfection. Now, she must pass the final test. Are you willing to witness her passage into perfection?"

"We are!"

The lips brushed against her head again.

"May your death be perfect!"

Anni trembled. The hands that held her legs apart readjusted themselves as a cushion was placed under her pelvis.

She sensed it before she felt it: the force of five fingers clutched together, the slow push of the index knuckle that slid past Anni's moist folds, followed by its kin into her already well-laved passage. Her muscles tensed as the fist began to move inside – up – down – and, slowly rotated as she bit her lips to keep from screaming... it was too much... too much...

The words died in Anni's throat as the fist paused to allow her, for a nano-second, to adjust to the invasion. She'd never been penetrated at this magnitude before. Anni slowly exhaled, relaxed her body around the now fully-engulfed fist. She felt the knuckles press against her cervix. It was like nothing Anni had ever experienced. Her years of vanilla, and then, bdsm-flavored sex with a handful of men couldn't match what she truly craved; this ruthless feminine appendage which stepped up the pace, drove into her with single-minded purpose, unceasing, unrelenting, yet, kept its shape - while it drove faster - and faster.

Anni reared up and down in time with fist that pounded into her. No one – until now - had ever brought Anni such satisfaction. She felt her soul unwind from her body as the Secret Word materialized from center of her being, traveled swiftly through her heart, and escaped, screaming, from her lips...

"PERFECTIBILIS!"
"PERFECTIBILIS!"
"PERFECTIBILIS!"

#

Anni awoke. Her eyes, blurry with tears, and free of the blindfold, struggled to make out the sea of pale smiling faces that surrounded her.

Two women came to her side, straightened her clothes, and helped her to her feet. Her legs shook. Were it not for the two women who braced her on either side, she would've fallen. She swayed for a moment. Tears streamed down her face. *What had happened? How was it she was still here?*

She looked looked herself over. Her pink strapless satin dress, corset, and white sash marked with the words "Prom Queen," were stained with her own juices and tears. Her wrists were branded with the pattern from the silken cords. Her feet, still shod in her Doc Martins, felt like lead weights. Her vagina was beyond sore.

"Come," a voice said. She looked up, and met the gaze of the voice who'd been by her side: The Leader, who now smiled at her. Anni took it all in; the long black hair, the bike chain draped around The Leader's ripe waist, the soft folds of her red flannel shirt.

Anni carefully take one hesitant step, then another. Her body was beyond exhausted. She had to concentrate all her focus on moving forward, until, at last, she stood in front of The Leader.

"Remove the trappings of her former life and clothe her in the garments of our sisterhood."

The two women quickly stripped Anni of the gown, sash, corset, and boots. She shivered, watched mutely as the women clothed her in new garments; relaxed jeans, wife-beater, fingerless wool gloves. Her boots were placed back on her feet, laces pulled and secured tight.

The Leader motioned to another woman, who came forward with a folded bundle. The Leader unwrapped the bundle, turned to Anni, and motioned for her to put out her arms.

36

"Here is your flannel shirt, the mark of our order. Wear it everywhere."

Anni put on the soft flannel blue shirt and buttoned it up to the collar.

The Leader handed Anni a small black wallet with a chain attached. Emblazoned on the leather was the silhouette of a mud-flap naked lady.

"Here is the wallet of our order. Keep all your necessities inside; your cash, dental dams, your health insurance card. Use it well, and keep it close, as a reminder of the new life you have been initiated into."

Anni fastened the chain to her jean loop, and, then stuffed the wallet in her back pocket.

"Only those willing to die to their former life – the life of the Beverly Hills housewife, the life of the Barbie Doll, are allowed in our number. Only those with the true heart's desire to be one of us are born with the secret word... the word you uttered at the time of your death... the only word that matters. Do you remember that word, Anni?"

Anni opened her mouth "P..."

"SHHH!" The Leader commanded. "That is a word sacred and secret, brought to us from Afra Sausenhofer-Weishaupt, the founder of our order, who grew bored and angry with her husband Adam's misogyny. From the shadows, Afra gathered together the wives and sisters and daughters of the Illuminati. These women formed a bond of sisterhood and came to know the real purpose of happiness: a fist into the heart of your very being."

"Whenever you hear a KD Lang song, we are there. Whenever you frequent a lesbian bar, we are there. Whenever you get the urge to put on high heels and go on a date with a man, we are there. We are always here, and you will never be alone."

The Leader held her fist to Anni's cheek, who could smell herself in the grip of those powerful fingers. Anni sighed with happiness. She was home.

"Welcome to our number, Sister! You've transcended the dichotomy. You've been reborn. You are now... *Perfect.*"

Alex S. Johnson currently resides in Northern California where he teaches college English. His work includes the novels *Bad Sunset* and *The Ghost Highway* (in progress) as well as the chapbooks *Matador of Mirrors* (Lucid Play, 2013), *The Doom Hippies, Doctor Flesh, Satanic Rites of the Nuns of St. Sophia* and *Black Tongues of the Illuminati* (Dynatox Ministries, 2013); and the full-length prose/poetry collection *The Death Jazz* (The Shwibly Press 2012). In May 2012 Johnson was a featured speaker at the world-famous Beyond Baroque poetry venue in Venice Beach. He has also published numerous articles on rock and heavy metal music in such magazines as *Metal Hammer*.

Stag

I don't mind working,
holding my ground intellectually,
artistically; but as a woman,
oh, God, as a woman I want to be dominated. — **Anaïs Nin**

I am the bow of my art
Strong enough to bend
Pliant and supple, good to release
An amphora of stags

Pin me to the tree
Of your blue movie
Shake me to the root
And let my shivered fruit
Quench your antler's thirst

Quivering on arrows of
Kind hurt, stunned suppliant
Your steel arouses my own
Silver on black, white as sperm
Black garters and Spanish cigarettes
I stand sit or move
At your cruel behest.

Henry and June

And gods caressed
His forehead, shivering
Whitmanic Kosmos to a plot
Of desire scribed on black sheets, we
Dance in splendor here without
Apology

And she too, despite the lies
Somewhere in her cockeyed breast
Beauty resides, thrashed steps of
That hideous puppet, her liquid
Voice, slurred with magical death.

There is no decision, I must
Love them both in
Splendors of succession, anoint
My lips with her musk and wear
Her salt, his tears, her glittering dust.

Les Petites Oiseaux

I wear the feathers of
This accidental bird
As the breathless school
Girls slip by my
Delirious arousal, mounting
The steps of betrayal,
The dark petals opening in silence
Of pierced roseate hum, an
Infamous priapic god.

Christine (CE) Jordan began life as a dancer and choreographer. She read a friend's rather middling elegy and said "Oh, I can do that!" and never looked back. She has been writing poetry since 1982, reading her work in public since 1992, and staging her own poems and stories since 1996. She has been published in *Blue Satellite, Beyond The Valley of the Contemporary Poets,* and *Armchair/Shotgun,* among others. Still, her passion is performing her words, using her theatre skills in new ways. She is appearing at Adapt Festival in Santa Barbara in a completely original work this August 2013.

Henry and Paul In My Head

Henry Miller, Anaïs Nin, Joni Mitchell, Erik Satie, Paul Klee, all saved my life. What was this life anyway, me at 17-years-old and stuck in Orange Country at a college that didn't even have enough space for me in the dorms back in 1968? I lived with a lady from my church. Jesus was used to saving folks I'm sure, but my old Setter back at home listened better than any human could during the worst year of my life, my senior year in High School.

Apostle Joni began to crack my hard shell of deep, deep depression when I got her song "Both Sides Now." I had never had a personal anthem til then. I remember sitting in Petey's living room, not a home, not a dorm, a kind of limbo worse than hell, and listening over and over, writing down the words, and finally beginning to see some light. College was a piece of cake for me, living not so much. From that day til a defining moment at The Hollywood Studio Club a year later, I relied on my new friends, Henry and Anaïs, to help and heal the newly minted artist.

How wonderful, how Bohemian, how not Orange County! I remember a similar ad hoc group of artists defining my life for the better in The Bloomsbury crowd, but in this tough and tender time, oh those two, those writers and lovers, blessed me with their magic lives! Miss Nin's books after books after books were like Miss Mitchell's songs, a literary anthem, therapy, hope, a winding of a gossamer chrysalis about the girl and the artist trying to form at the very same time.

I was fortunate to take a class called "The Creative Process," while at UCI that Freshman year of mine, where Henry Miller was one of the subjects studied. Part of his process was to place his writing desk smack in the middle of a room, treating it as a sacred altar, surrounded by sacred space. Yes, I had read all his steamy books in high school, so hearing about the abject spirituality of this amazing man treated me to a personal coup.

I began to collect my own artist stories which I could learn from them. I will always be able to see that desk of his shimmering and pulsing in that hallowed space. Of course he had his lovers, but the sacred is art, and art is the sacred. I have never lost that belief, and Henry Miller, misunderstood messiah taking all our sins upon him, still holds court in that upper room. Later, as a full on poet, his book of essays, *Wisdom of the Heart*, clearly showed to me a true philosopher, never finding such wisdom in the works of the usual philosophers. Miller's quote about how the world is neutral, neither out to destroy you nor to laud you, and how we are then completely free to write our own histories, unburdened by other minds' fears and apprehensions, is my talisman, forever and now.

That Freshman class of bedrock artists, Miller, Nin, Satie, all Dada, all Gymnopedie, and young as we ourselves were, are my first, best teachers. Appearing because I was told to read something, but quite quickly knowing what to read next and next and next, my friend Anaïs Nin lead the class. The lives of the artists came next, living with me there in Hollywood, a true Bohemian berg. My Paul Klee finally freed me from the shell, transparent but solid sphere I traveled around in through the universe, a mute looking out on all the rough jollity. Seeing and identifying with a painting I cannot find now of space travelers (me) cracking open their ship (me) and soaring away, free from debilitating doubt and depression, enough to get a foothold on earth, was the very moment I trusted I might grow up whole and many-faceted.

So you see, Miss Nin, your influence on Henry, who influenced who knows who, but especially the poet searching for nothing less than the meaning of life, provide life's primers for the women and the artists... always.

Michelle Angelini - *Hibiscus*

Alystyre Julian is a multi-genre writer of screenplays, prose, and film reviews, and is at work on a feature documentary about "Outrider" Poet Anne Waldman.

She has an MFA in Writing from Bard College, and is a certified yoga instructor. She has worked in education and publishing, and is transitioning into film/TV media. She often documents writers and nature, and is currently drawn to Argentine Tango. Originally from Chapel Hill, North Carolina, Alystyre has lived and worked in New York City for two decades. Her first job in Manhattan was at the Gotham Book Mart, where she collected first editions of Anais Nin stamped by the author.

From the early journals of Alystyre Julian (mid–1990's):

Oct. 3 New York.

    He was unfastening her jeans while she sat in a chair in front of his chair. They were on the roof surrounded by no one. His back was to me and she had not seen me yet. I knew she would notice if I moved. She looked like the actress Beatrice Dalle. They are very young. I move and when I glance back they have seen me. She is now putting him off. She is now self-conscious. They talk and he tries and she makes him hesitate, wait. They put their arms around each other's neck. She kisses in his left ear. I turn my position opposite, so my perspective is not direct. I leave. One last glance and they have noticed my leaving, my window shutting.

Alystre Julian - *Here*

30 June Paris Café/Gare D'Austerlitz

I am floating. The air is soft. The rain soft. All the hardness of New York and blankness for lack of a better word is gone. Signs and words pleasant to see. Fill in hostility for one of the blanks in the blankness of America. I am already more at peace. I cried as I entered the plane to come here. I had been experiencing a crisis. It began to let go as I got on the plane, added to the realization that I would land in France. I look in the Air France magazine and the country of France resembles a heart. Raining a lot. Still beautiful & soft. I want to leave America, I want to move here. Je suis seule. I love the language. Already, I know I love many things about this heart-shaped country.

In New York, a lot of the time I was feeling anxiety and it was aging me. It was coming from directions outward, inward, and catty corners. No sense of continuous movement. A bit of a sense of flow intermittently helped but I grow tired easily there. Here, there seems like hope & freshness in the softness provided I also match this softness from myself to it. I am having a stop–start flow of thoughts. I am watching what I think, write. Why. I am about to take a train going south in the rain.

Dream 7 JuilletHotel La Louisiane

I go into a room and with a knife, slice my legs at the thighs until they separate from me. There is no pain. I am lying down with my legs off. In a hotel. I feel my legs detached from me. I feel the limbs. I reach down under the and slide my body back onto my legs, using my hands to re-attach. Somehow I get out of and stand up. The blood coagulates and sticks enough to stand on cut off legs. It feels like being on stilts, a bit wobbly. Not messy though since the blood is contained where I had made the separation. I lay back down, and the next time I look at my legs, they are miraculously stitched on already. I had not been aware of them being stitched. The stitches were clean ones and healing had already begun. I had on pants, jeans maybe, on leaving the room and walking through the hotel restaurant. Also I see the boots clearly that Beatrice Dalle wears in Jarmusch's film "Night on Earth". She stands on an island in the middle of the streets at about 4 a.m. And waves a taxi down, though she is blind. She goes in the taxi to the Seine to walk. She senses much more than the cab driver who challenges her vision. My seeing the boots is part of my dream.

48

Alystre Julian - *Tango Shoes Aside*

Alystre Julian -
Tulip Heart

I have ridden the big Ferris wheel, the Grand Roue, three times. The last time I received a throne of my own. From the height of the arc, all of Paris, from Sacre – Coeur to Montparnasse to the Tour Eiffel to the Louvre could be viewed. The wheel itself was the smoothest and cleanest machine ride I've ever taken. The whole amusement park is just that, a park. Clean and magical. Leaving I knew distinctly that the Grand Roue was an image for my solar plexus. The spokes of the wheel leading from my heart, the center. There is excitement in the air here. Possibly pre–Bastille day. A Parisian woman on a bicycle with a sequined hat and sequined basket. An accordion playing. Piano behind me. Festive. I give the accordion player all my last change. A mix of the present and of the past running smoothly side by side and intertwining here. There is respect for the past influences, history, life. The piano heating up behind with clapping, and some be–bop. The Louvre tonight for only an hour. The Mona Lisa was alive to me. She was more alluring and subtlety beautiful than I had suspected. There was no end to looking at her portrait. I wished that I had spend a little time every day there, discovering. At the Louvre and the Rodin, there were young men and women sketching the famous and more obscure works. This caught my interest as an exercise. Not for me to draw, but the way I stop sometimes and sketch words, from what its in front of me. When the main galleries closed, I went outside the svelte transparent pyramid, and walked through the rows of water, running and spouting from the fountain shoots. I sat down and snuck my feet in the cold water. Heaven, coolness. I could have ravished the fountain I loved it so much at that instant. I loved the clean, bare space surrounding. I walked on the periphery of the low fountain wall, the edges, and tossed the water with my feet. I kept in my gaze the Ferris wheel behind the pyramid, really through the pyramid, and the blue, white, pink open sky just before a fast twilight.

Marie Lecrivain is a writer, photographer, and the editor of *poeticdiversity: the litzine of Los Angeles*. Her work has appeared in various journals, including *Cuib Nest Nido, Illumen, Maintanent, The Los Angeles Review, Poetry Salzburg Review, The Shwibly*, and others. Her poetry collection, *Love Poems... Yes... REALLY... Love Poems* (© 2013 Sybaritic Press), is available through Amazon.com.

In Appreciation of Anaïs Nin

Life shrinks or expands in proportion to one's courage. - **Anaïs Nin**

Today, I found your words on a shelf,
demurely clothed in a dust jacket,
and politely crowned a first edition.
Holding you in my hands,
I realize that there was,
and,
never will be anyone
like you,
the perfect fusion
of apocrypha and holiness
woven into page after page
of your life story,
pouring forth from the delta of Venus
all women want to find within themselves;
the words and tales and faces
and lives and loves
flew forth from your soul
like so many little birds
and, now, the veil has been lifted...
I have my own truths to tell,
and, I thank you.

(previously published in *Poetry Super Highway*, 2013)

My Soul as Jaguar

We travel, some of us forever,
to seek other states, other lives, other souls. - **Anaïs Nin**

Today, I noticed a series of brown spots
that mapped their way down the backs of my legs
and arms. Alarmed, my stomach tied in knots
as I imagined the pitiful dregs
of my youth drowned in a flood of umber
colored old age. Then, I laughed. This is the time
where alchemy does its best work. The number
of freckles and age spots don't matter. The grime
is a testament - a chrysalis - for what
comes next - the distillation of my soul,
a time to sleep until the outer shell is cut
away and the true Me leaps out, joyous, whole,
and free. With a touch of karmic agility
I'll spring like a jaguar - into infinity.

Marie Lecrivain - *Isis*

Cynthia Linville has lived in London, New York, San Francisco, and outside of Washington DC, but keeps coming back to live in her hometown of Sacramento. She has taught in the English Department at California State University, Sacramento, since 2000 and has served as Managing Editor of *Convergence: an online journal of poetry and art* since 2008. She is active in the local poetry scene, hosting readings, and reading with the group Poetica Erotica as well as on her own. Her book of collected poems, *The Lost Thing*, is available from Cold River Press.

Unmasking

You revealed yourself in little pieces –
the corner of your smile
a Jungian sketch
a thousand vinyl albums
six-year-old set lists.

You brought me to your home –
not "loft" as in tiled floors
softly lit ferns
and pastel furniture,
but makeshift concrete, drywall, and 2x4s.

You threaded me through your collection
of guitars and photographer's props –
red boxing gloves
pink elbow gloves
and rubber Frankenstein masks.

After we made out
on your sagging green velveteen couch
you led me up steep, splintery stairs
(handcuffs dangling from the iron-rod rail)
to your thick mattress

where I let you undress me
then dress me up again
in silky leopard skin
in rough leather
in nothing but a feather fan.

I let you show me
who I am.

Joseph F. Mailander has written fiction, cultural criticism, and poetry from 1981 forward. His most recent novel *The Strong God Glittering*, a meditation on sex and gender ambiguity, was especially formed by the works of Proust, Lawrence Durrell, Anaïs Nin, and the academic work of Judith Butler. Mailander's fiction, cultural criticism and poetry have appeared in many print and online publications. He now divides his time between Los Angeles and San Luis Obispo, California.

Diana and Delilah

(from *The Strong God Glittering*)

About two hours or so later, it becomes vaguely sexual between the two of them. The girls bear-hugging each other, with Delilah always initiating, and Diana offering a cautious amount of affection in return.

Then Delilah wants to see whose arms are smaller, hers or Diana's.

Diana is giggly and playing along and Delilah drags her to the bathroom mirror to compare.

Something goes on, I don't know what, but Diana calls me in to do the determining. My guess is that Delilah has become a little too physical for Diana's comfort.

I enter. Here we are, the three of us in the long bathroom, with the sink-to-ceiling mirror and Diana's nude paintings from ages ago; the two girls standing as spoons, Delilah behind Diana, with the right shoulders jutting out towards the mirror. Both girls are only wearing underwear; their summer dresses are draped over the shower rod.

Now I am wrapping my fingers around Delilah's lower bicep, then reaching across her to wrap them around Diana's, drawn in once again by Delilah, pulling both Diana and me closer to her.

It turns out Delilah's are smaller, but only because Diana's are far more muscular; after all, there were years of archery, and now she trains with shadow boxers in a class three days a week, and the class is taught by an angry jarhead who has had two heart attacks since his iffy discharge from the Marines. Diana's biceps are tiny but they feel like a man's.

And that's where we stand for the next twenty minutes: in the bathroom, before the mirror. Nobody is anxious to leave; we are all looking at each other in the mirror in every possible combination. Delilah doesn't look at me much, however; she's looking mostly at Diana. Diana is mostly looking at herself; I will later recognize she is looking at herself the way she looks at herself when we make love. She acts sweet, incogitant; she doesn't want to feel pretty when standing next to Delilah, the exotic hothouse specimen. She doesn't look at me at all, but she does steal glances of Delilah, and she doesn't seem afraid to do so.

I am truly shocked. They are standing as mannequins in their underthings; they have both forgotten about me. I am imperceptible.

Other parts of their bodies are discussed but not measured. Diana complains about her own breasts. The breast contest we can all see is not a contest at all, as Diana is small and Delilah is large. As for half the afternoon I have been able to see the way the bottom of Delilah's bra is cutting into her ribs, I have a good idea as to precisely how wide the margin is. Delilah offers Diana little consolation, in fact none at all. Nor do I. Frankly, I do not care. At this moment, I only want to look at Delilah's eyes from six inches away.

And I am indeed mostly looking at Delilah, not Diana, in the mirror. I am hoping to catch her eyes for some meaningful duration. I do not succeed more than once every two minutes or so. The girls carry on with their scherzo for no real sake other than to extend it.

Delilah suddenly breaks the music in half and says, "Look at us!" Then she flails her ceaselessly flailing arms to full extent behind us, while leaning forward, to say again, "Let's get on with it!" and then she hugs both of us.

The three of us stand together, now me behind the two girls, all of us with arms wrapped around each other and pressing in closely. The sexual tension mounts like electrical power coming to a household after an outage: noises, lights blinking on, durable goods suddenly humming after a long dormancy.

This is the cornice of our relationship to date; certainly for me, likely for Delilah, maybe for all. I'm shocked—and hoping to tell someone—that Diana has gone this far without turning back. But I should not be shocked, because I learned early on that Diana does not turn back.

I am also lost. I do not even know what would be next. But I do know: if Delilah had kissed Diana—she couldn't—she has a small cold sore—I would have kissed Diana too, and both Delilah and I probably would have begged her to play even just a little more. It would be quite a scene from there. I do not know a lot about how this works, but Diana is beyond extremely naive with regards to intimacy with women, even though she is the constant target of sapphists, which likely makes her even more attractive to Delilah, who has just stolen away with a moment that she pushed for and that became hers to steal. But even Delilah, who initiates so much play, is not abundantly sexually experienced, as she constantly moans to both of us.

60

I do feel that it is my partner Diana whom both Delilah and I want to do something more. I feel for a moment that both Delilah and I are on the verge of doing something a little more intimate to Diana, but don't know what we should do. Whatever it is, it doesn't happen.

Or it could be simply a case of three people standing in front of a bathroom mirror, measuring two women's biceps on a Sunday afternoon.

Hastily, as might water nymphs suddenly discovered in a forest, the two undressed girls reach for their dresses; Diana takes hers from the bar with one easy downwards pull of the hands, and Delilah, the visitor, carefully reaches up to the bar, stretching her legs and her bottom and rising on he toes, to fetch her own sheer piece. Then they hustle into their dresses, and then they continue to talk about how good they look together, and look to me with some pity, and then we all hug again; it is four o'clock in the afternoon.

M. Frias May lives near the gateway to Big Sur with his wife, Juanita, and four-legged son, Rico. He's down to two-and-half cigarettes a day and still gives money to panhandlers. He cooks, does his own laundry, and plays a pretty good version of "Political Science." He likes tequila, in a snifter. Sometimes, he gets published. And sometimes he can remember his dreams.

Nin in the Afterlife

Heater goes on
When winter steps on spring
Walk with me
Keep an eye out for crows
In gull's feathers
Impulses that do what they please
Like cats
Disemboweling the unknowable
Now
Open your mouth

Blonde in a Red Tunnel

Do not
Go home
The mollusk in a past life has
Slipped off the rock, has a
Future for you:
Cable TV blonde
Pro in high heels
In a red tunnel of blue voices:
I'm off even when I'm on
Surf and Cha-Cha
Her chosen smile tolerated by
God's mysterious ways

Marie Lecrivain - *Vagina Dentata*

Ruth Nolan is a Southern California native who grew up in a remote area of the Mojave Desert and is professor of creative writing at College of the Desert. A former helicopter hotshot firefighter, she is also award-winning poet and writer who blogs about culture and arts in the desert for award-winning KCET Artbound, LA and for Heyday Books. She is the editor of *No Place for a Puritan: the literature of California's deserts* (Heyday Books 2009,) and a contributor to Heyday's landmark anthology, *Inlandia: A Literary Journey through Southern California's Inland Empire*. Her poetry and prose writing have appeared recently or are forthcoming in *San Diego Poetry Annual 2013; Beyond the Arroyo: the Southern California Haiku Study Group 2012 Anthology; Fresh Ink; New California Writing 2011* (Heyday); *Night Becomes the Night - Los Angeles Noir Poetry; Crow and Raven: California Writers on Crows and Ravens; Inlandia: A Literary Journey; Pacific Review; Phantom Seed; Coachella Valley Archaeology Society Magazine; Tin Cannon,* and *Ghost Republic.* She lectures widely in academic and other public settings on issues related to California desert literature, culture, and conservation.

Forbidden Fruit

*I only believe in intoxication, in ecstasy, and when ordinary life shackles me,
I escape, one way or another. No more walls"* -**Anaïs Nin**

The missing ovary at seventeen
did not seem as edible to me
as the sweet California oranges
drooping on belly-shaped trees.

The girl in the other bed cried
all night on her side of the room
because she couldn't have kids
and I joked with the cute male

night nurse in my codeine haze,
imagining sweet drippings on my
tongue, stretch marked rinds on the
floor, mouthfuls of bitter seeds,

the part you spit out afterwards,
fleshy strips clinging to your teeth
white blossoms cupped in your open
hands, then floating down to earth.

What Rises

"How wrong is it for a woman to expect the man to build the world she wants, rather than to create it herself?" -**Anaïs Nin**

You, in your stripped-down kitchen,
essential tools in knowing hands:
hammer, skill saw, tape measure
the mouthful of blunt-tipped nails.

Me, hair blowing in the open air,
convertible top rolled down this
desert night, swollen orange moon
embellishing my rounded thighs.

While you re-model and plan,
shift the room around and put
the refrigerator against the other
wall, I change gears in a different

time zone in the desert west. I braid
my hair, untangle the ropy knots
of mangled string, while you cut
and glue and keep the wild puppy

from strangling on its chewed toys.
And you have patience to deal
with this: unruly pets, disorder
in the kitchen, a woman roaming

deserts and mountains on loan,
hammering the center of sunrise
to her heart. You work, I climb
another harsh peak and sleep late,

nailed to bed in fading moonlight.
I awaken, hungry, and your kitchen
will soon be in place, dog in cage,
the sun smoothing the beveled night.

Marie Lecivain - *Warshagen*

Angel Uriel Perales is a poet and writer currently residing in Valley Village, CA. He also works as a broadcast technician for a television network. If you are interested in reading more of his work, please visit his literary website at www.rumrazor.com.

Iced Water on the Table

We don't see things are they are, we see them as we are. - **Anaïs Nin**

She wore her best sleepwear, a silk bra and panties inset with a floral design. She purchased them at Target, the brand: Self Expressions. When she looked at herself in the changing room mirror she thought she looked good, slim, the silk was comfortable and the fit was kind to her figure, so she bought the economical set. Now as she slipped into a little black dress, she felt confident about the date. She applied maroon lipstick.

He paid attention to his underwear as well, made sure the jockey briefs smelled clean and no holes appeared anywhere. He had not bought new clothes of any kind in two years because he didn't have the extra money. And every time he thought he should make a trip to some department store at some mall somewhere to get new jeans or work slacks, something else always came up, a new clutch plate for the car, a change in his health insurance premium, he always had to adjust. Last month he meant to replace his scuffed work boots but he had to buy a new vacuum cleaner, of all things. This month he was spending his extra cash mostly on the week before Valentine's Day, on dry cleaners, a car wash, full tank of gasoline, haircut. He splashed on an extra dollop of aftershave. His old suit and tie was black with a touch of red.

Her uterine fibroid bothered her during dinner. She reached down inconspicuously and pressed down on her lower stomach to ease the pain. She tried to concentrate on the story he was regaling but all her pending menopause worries flooded through her body. She flushed with heat and her cervix cramped. She became breathless. He paused in storytelling. She brushed hair away from her face and wanly smiled. He continued with his story. She drank some wine.

The first recommended treatment when the fibroid was discovered was to try to shrink the tumor with medication but the side effects had been disastrous. She tolerated the second round of pills much better but they had so far proven ineffective. She had to change her long-standing contraceptive, also had to begin ingesting an iron supplement to deal with anemia. And the pain is severe enough to the point where she has to take ibuprofen daily. The doctor warned if she got pregnant her treatment would have to be changed completely. She laughed at the thought of pregnancy

71

but the doctor assured her stranger things have happened. In fact, this week, the week before Valentine's Day, the doctor suggested a hysterectomy, since she was only a few years away from the end of her monthly cycles. The fibroid would only calcify further until the natural regression after menopause, so she needed to lower her estrogen levels, get off birth control. She said she needed time to decide, not because of some nostalgic desire for a child, such a possibility died within her a long time ago and, again, the thought of accidental pregnancy was preposterous, but for the simple want of establishing intimacy in her new relationship before taking away the option of sex for a month or longer. She felt as if she had to prove herself to her new man.

He had the bad habit of eating ice. He did not know why he did this, crunch ice, something he has always done like a nervous rabbit. When the waiter placed iced water on the table after they sat down, he immediately took a swig, swirled some ice around his mouth like a lozenge. The third cube he bit into cracked his lower back molar, he heard the crack, he felt the crack, and a hard piece of enamel slipped to the back of his throat, made him gag, he almost vomited. He sat up coughing, grabbed the napkin from his lap, and spit the piece out. She asked if he was alright, he nodded, drank some more water, then examined the napkin. The top of the tooth was grayish white, the underside black. He pursed his mouth and used his tongue and felt over what was left of the molar, the front side was strong and in place but along the back other pieces of the tooth were loose and threatening to dislodge.

Now he was paranoid to chew. And he had ordered a sirloin with all the fixings. Anytime food touched the cracked tooth he inwardly winced in pain. He resorted to eating from the opposite side of his mouth, then decided he looked weird masticating in that manner. Eventually, and embarrassed, he quit eating altogether. This meant he had to fill up the time with endless chatter.

What he talked about during the interminable dinner, he had no idea. His mind was racing with doomsday scenarios. He could not afford a dentist, not now, and he just knew he would lose his tooth. Without the money to afford a cap, he would have to live with a huge gap inside his mouth. All his teeth would, in time, push into each other and maybe even into the hole extraction. He would have gaps between all his lower teeth. Or maybe he would grow a huge unsightly keloid inside his mouth, a purple keloid. And he would be at risk for sinus infections, he read once of somebody who had actually died in such a gruesome way. Of a more immediate concern was the rising heat inside his mouth, he felt his cracked tooth again with his tongue and, sure enough, the spot was feverish.

He drank all the iced water on the table. Unconsciously, or not, she couldn't be sure, after he finished his glass, he casually reached over, grabbed her glass and drank her water. He ate her ice, drank her water. Then he asked for more water, exclusively for him, not any for her, he was insistent on ice, and when the water arrived, he drank all the water and ate all the ice. He talked and did not eat any of his food on his plate other than a few small bites. The water, though, she would remember the water, the ice, his thirst, and the speed by which he drove her back to her home. Her fibroid hurt.

She peed blood. Before bed, before taking off her makeup with cotton balls dipped in baby oil, after folding and putting away her bra but before sleeping in her panties, and before slipping into a simple and nondescript flannel nightgown over those same panties, her urine was pink tinged with yellow. The nightlight bulb in her bedroom blew out in the middle of the night. She did not notice.

Do not seek the because- in love there is no because, no reason, no explanation, no solutions. - **Anaïs Nin**

Flash fiction writer **BC Petrakos** has had her work published in various literary journals all over the world. Her original screenplay, "Stanley," has been optioned, and several of her flash fiction stories have been made into short films. She has two books published by Sybaritic Press, *Country Fixins,* and *Stories From The Inside Edge.* She is thrilled to be in this anthology, and included in the company of such great writers.

The Evolution and Reincarnation of Anaïs Nin

Charles had a nanny, a nanny who was fat and round and loved to talk on the phone.

He was delivered to the park, as usual, at 10 am, after the parents drank coffee, after he was fed star-shaped white flour and sugar bits with milk that tasted like water. After the long conversation between the adults, the list of instructions to his nanny, Charles was strapped in his dark blue stroller for what seemed like an eternity. As he waited, he realized his nanny dressed him in mismatched clothes again, which troubled him today for no reason at all. Today, he felt different in his three-year-old body. Today he was irritated, the parents irritated him, and the nanny irritated him. He tried to be patient, tried to ignore the buckled-in feeling of the stroller, the adult voices in a language that was graceless, the mismatched clothes and his realization that there was a tremendous lack of style in his life. He did not know why this was important, but today it seemed very important.

Once they reached the park, the nanny unbuckled Charles from his stroller. He ran full speed to the slide, and, it was there that he had the strangest idea; that his legs were small and, somehow, not his legs.

This was an unusual idea from a part of his mind that was not his mind, and made no sense at all.

He slid down the slide and looked at his feet. He saw his feet also seemed tiny, and his shoes were dirty, which bothered him for no reason, and had never bothered him before. Charles sat at the end of the slide instead of running to the swing as he always did. He held up his hands to the sun and looked at them closely. In that weird part of his mind, the part of his mind that wasn't him, that was bothering him today, he had the thought that his hands were not his hands, and his feet were not his feet. Charles strangely expected to see long white fingers and painted red nails, to see longer legs that were different then what he had now. He ignored his strange idea and ran to the swings. His fat nanny sat on the bench and shouted something to him in Spanish, which he understood better then the English his mother spoke. And for some reason the sound of the language comforted him, even though her version of words were rough and not quite right.

All day he played, just like any day before, but this day things were not perfectly right. His face was not his face, his voice could not use words as he knew somehow could, and when he saw the other children, specifically the little girls, he felt a sad feeling.

His nanny did not give him lunch that day. Instead, when he flew off the merry go-round and started to cry, she gave him a sucker.

He did not want a sucker, he did not want her to wrap her fat arms around him and shush him, he did not want to stop crying. He wanted to remember.

He wanted to remember the longer legs, the red fingernails, the words. He wanted to remember why he felt sorry for the little girls, and wanted to know why his body was not his body, and wanted to remember where he was before. He felt like "before" was someplace wonderful, horrific, heartbreaking and full of adventure. Charles felt he knew things, and he had been tricked into forgetting them.

When it was time to go home, as usual, he had to take a bath. As his nanny took off his clothes, he looked in the mirror, watched her take off his sweater, his pants, his shorts. He stood in the mirror and looked at himself. The eyes in his mind laughed.

There was a woman's voice in his head, a thousand thoughts about love, men, and dreams. A woman's voice flooded his mind; her name was strange, she wasn't possessing him, but he was remembering her. Somehow, in a few seconds, something inside him knew he was out-living her, he would outlive her voice, he would forget it, wash its poetry from his hands in his *Mr. Bubble* bath. It was a strange day, but, as he got into the tub he grabbed his "willie." He loved his willie because it was the most important thing in the world! This action changed everything. His willie *was* him!

The part of Charles that was a writer, long ago, that lived in Echo Park, Paris, Spain, the part of Charles that before, was longing to please, longing to touch, longing to express, would not live in his future, not wear his blue jeans, not play basketball, and fight. The part of Charles that he was remembering had exactly what it wanted this time. Charles had a willie; he was not a woman, or a girl.

Charles was now in the process of quenching the thirst of his memory of her. She would have to submit. In his future, he would not like to write, find or look for love, not care for anything enough to distress him. He would not be distressed in this life. He would shoot guns, play sports and become indifferent, shallow, entitled, and happy. There would be no insights, no lectures, no moments of

76

conflict, infidelity, incest, sexual intrigue, or longing. Charles would be comfortable. In short, he would evolve to independence. Charles would be ordinary; male, happy, confused by, and avoid drama, and at all costs. He would be able to make himself happy at a golf course, or a *Three Stooges* marathon. He had had in his consciousness already experienced being the woman in his other part of his other mind, he had experienced raw emotion, and now, he would move on. Charles had a willie; it was the most important thing, the most powerful thing. That woman with the pen in hand, the hand on cock, the mouth to kiss, unable to reach fullness, would be full at last be complete because now she had her own willie at long last! Charles would live an unexpressed-white-male-born-to-a-Lawyer-and-Interior-Designer-with-a-fat-round-Nanny-in-the-mean-streets-of-Pacific-Palisades kind of life.

Charles would stop thinking about the strange feelings. He would kick his dog, bite his nanny, take off his towel and run into the front yard naked. For now, he would show the other voice that other life, that being a boy was better, always better. Charles had what Anaïs needed to be happy... Charles had his own perfect willie, so, he could ignore poetry, insight, and longing. He was going to live the life of the stranger she never met with desires so easily taken care of it would be a gift. She would accept it, as the strangest dream and meld into the perfection she longed for.

A Mid-West native from Cleveland, Ohio, **J.R. Phillips** has spent the majority of his years in Los Angeles, California. His father was an immigrant from the U.K. & his mother was second generation Irish American. He attended university courses at University of Oregon, Cal Ploy San Luis Obispo and received his undergraduate degree from the Cal State University Northridge where he studied under the guidance of famed California poet Ann Stanford. He is currently enrolled in the Graduate Program at Antioch University. He has recently published two books of poetry from Red Luna Press— *Living in Lotus Land* and *A Mirage of Suspended Gardens*. Three earlier publications are no longer in print. A handful of select poems were published in the Centennial Edition of *The Wallace Stevens Journal*, *Wormwood Review,* and an anthology entitled *Men in the Company of Women*. He is co-host and founder of the Valley Poets East Reading series in Studio City, California. Mr. Phillips makes his living as an investment advisor in one of the largest California-based investment banks in the U.S.

Medusa

It's alright for a woman to be, above all, human.
I am a woman first of all. — **Anaïs Nin**

You came to me
Expecting something different
From what I am.
Medusa, you call me
Sprouting serpents from my head.
My eyes trouble you, you said.
Of my stares and gazes
You have been warned.
All those sirens and vixens,
Those harlots and whores
Luring the pure-hearted and the noblest
Of men.
You expected something different from what I am.
I am just a woman
Rejecting that which too many women
Have come to accept:
To be both worshiped and reviled,
To be hunted like prey,
To be used and vilified for our sex.
I am just a woman
Neither demon nor deity,
Neither saint nor sacred muse.
I am just a woman,
That part of man a man must mirror his shield
To recognize.
You who dare not face me,
Who hold me by my hair in your outstretched hand
Beware my deadly stare,
Beware the woman of man you covet and fear.

Hattie Quinn is a Thelemite, a deviant, a writer, and a bookseller, recently relocated to the Pacific Northwest, where she can listen to the rain while she writes or plays with her two feline companions, Agent Uno and Simon, except during the summer, when there is just too much damned sunshine going on.

Concentrate on the Poetry

To F.D., understanding friend and fellow destroyer of walls.

When the bell rings signaling us to turn off electronics, I smile as I remember the trip that rekindled sex. I was jaded, as likely to pass as I was to accept, assuming I'd never know the intimate connection of lovers. Not so. I was going east for a trade-show to show off the company's wares while attendees groped mine. At forty, yoga had done its work to keep me trim, though I was more statuesque than lithe. We 'booth babes' keep them coming, hoping to catch a glimpse of thigh under a skirt while perusing the latest in biometric devices.

On came notice that I had to put away my e-book. Worse, I had forgotten my book and had already read this month's airline magazine. What to do until use was cleared? I looked, finding a fellow 'babe,' I recognized as Rose, reading, and noticed there was another book in her bag. I took it, asking permission while not waiting for it. She blushed, making freckles dance across porcelain skin, nodded, lowering her eyes to page, letting her copper curls fall forward. This must be good to inspire such a reaction; oh, and it was... *Delta of Venus* by Anaïs Nin.

Healing began with these words:

> "Sex loses all its... magic when it becomes explicit, mechanical... It becomes a bore. You have taught us... how wrong it is not to mix it with emotion, hunger, desire... deeper relationships that change its color, flavor, rhythms, intensities."

A perfect summation of my sex life, mechanical. Where was my hunger? I reflected on recent affairs with a blur of reps in gray suits. Furtive encounters, consisting of partial disrobing and curt impalement upon engorged manhood, racing to climax.

I get wet on demand. I masturbate often, a fantasy enough to cause my juices to flow. Why not with others? Why more of the "wham, grrr, thank you, sir"?

> "You do not know what you are missing by your microscopic examination of sexual activity to the exclusion of... the fuel that ignites it. Intellectual, imaginative, romantic, emotional. This is what gives sex... its aphrodisiac elements... You are... draining its blood."

Was I?

> "The source of sexual power is curiosity, passion...
> Sex must be mixed with tears, laughter... jealousy,
> envy, all the spices of fear, foreign travel...
> stories... dancing... wine."

I meditated on that which would elevate me from mundane to divine. I fell asleep, dreaming of sex, blood, and wine, and was awoken by the plane landing. Rose was gone when I looked, so I tucked her book under my arm, promising to return it at first opportunity, which proved to be at the end of the show. Tired from smiling all weekend, bum sore from pinches, all I wanted was a bath and a bottle of champagne.

We found each other in the elevator behind a mass of manly, ex-marine types in office casual. She was pressed back, stepped on my toes, and I yelped. She turned and I was lost in her stunning green eyes.

"My book thief," she teased. I managed an apology as she shifted around to face me, bosom to bosom.

"I will forgive you, if I may pick it up tonight. I won't go another night without love," she spoke huskily, breath warm upon my skin. I nodded, barely able to extract a key-card from pocket. "I'm going to order room service and draw a bath," I whispered, "Room 418."

Her face lit up like an angel, but there was something of the devil in her eye, and I wondered what I had done. Returning to my suite, I threw off my clothes, grabbed waterproof vibrator, and filled the tub. I didn't hear her over the sounds of whirring and my delight; I am a screamer. My body writhed, water splashing her bare feet. I opened my eyes and there she was, glorious and naked as when she rose from the sea upon a giant shell, Botticelli's *Venus*, divine love in woman-form.

I blushed, emerging, and she toweled me as I dripped water and sexual fluids, slowly rising up my legs with the plush cotton. I closed them modestly, and heard, "to quote the Basque, 'I will make you open there.'" I knew that she meant to force them open, using mouth instead of brush. She kissed my delta and I relented, legs, then lips parting. Alabaster skin a beautiful contrast to tanned flesh, I watched her fingers enter my pussy as she licked my swollen clitoris with the skill of a master.

Meeting to kiss, tasting myself upon her mouth, clenching her tresses, needing to envelop her, she slipped from my grasp, beckoning me. I gasped and she silenced me. I complied, following to the bed where she posed me: legs spread, on pillow, fingers holding lips open for reception.

Sweet kisses on thigh, on quivering flesh; one hand caressed my breast, pinching my nipple harder as it excited me, while the other entered me, one finger at a time, with rising intensity as my twat expanded; stopping my squirming with offhand, gently probing wet finger into my ass, my body convulsed with orgasm. She looked from between my legs, impish smile matching glint in eye.

"Don't move," she ordered, going out, returning with two glasses of champagne and a jar of cream with which she slathered my pussy and her hand. I was naive enough to misunderstand until she was filling me with her spreading fingers, stretching, as if to prepare my cunt for more.

Slowly she worked, widening me, nearly bringing me to yet abating climax. I shivered with wantonness, resigned to take whatever, which turned out to be her fist. Her entire balled hand, moving in and out, pushing me beyond limits as I conformed to her ministrations. I left my body, barely noticing the flood of my come, transcendent.

I knew poetry again, trembling in awe of this young fiend, yet gave myself whole. I was revived, and won't settle for the blur, seeking instead the soul of an artist and that mischievous sparkle, ever eager.

C. R. Resetarits' latest poetry appears in *New Writing: The International Journal for the Practice and Theory of Creative Writing*, *Solo Novo*, *dirtcakes*, and *Clockhouse Review*. Her essay on "Emerson in Paris" will appear in *Paris in American Literature: On Distance as a Literary Resource*, ed. Jeffrey Herlihy and Vamsi K. Koneru (Rowman & Littlefield, 2013).

Shell Shores

I heard the sound of the sea in a shell in the crook of your arm while you played cradle to my prodigal restlessness; always, go-go, more-more, heave-ho, always, but just for a moment I stop, eyes closed, ears full of roar while you stayed at breast, neck, dip of spine as long as you wanted, always less is more, pare-pare, consommé and we were in that way which is our rich stock and trade. Still the sound of the sea in a shell in the crook of your arm was alone in my head but for you who hovered as moon to tides and rhythms and afternoons skinborne to far ephemeral shores.

(Previously published in the UK journal *Parameter*, Spring 2006)

Apryl Skies is a 2012 Pushcart nominee and award-winning author of *A Song Beneath Silence* (Readers Favorite 2012), *Skye the Troll & Other Fairy Tales* (Best Poetry book of 2010 by Muses Review) and was honored by the American Pixel Academy with the 2010 Gold Pixie Award for her animated feature film *Polyphony*.

Skies exhibits natural talent with poetry, photography, and canvas. Her devotion to written & spoken word is expressed with a quiet intensity.

Apryl's musings have been published in print & online internationally, and she has been featured at some of the most prominent venues throughout Los Angeles.

Impressions of Exotic Fruit

And I always dreamed of being awakened with a caress like this. - **Anaïs Nin**

I.
Little birds sang of you
wrapped in Egyptian linen
as your beautiful eyes close
somewhere in Morocco.

Where vibrant tiles
and empress dates lie
on a table painted in still-life.
Art ready to be devoured.

He wishes to paint you
with soft brushes of
light and shadow,
draw lines of your landscape
in charcoal smudges.

"I am dying." He says.

And I want to love
every woman within reach

--out of reach--

while there is still time...

Embrace her flaws,
hold silent her scent
captive within dream,
paint her soul
which remains a pale sketch
in a colorless dream.

Use blue ink
to capture her words left unsaid
where her story remains
unfinished as bone.

"Love is never simple,
it shouldn't be
and I am dying." He says.

And a woman deserves
to be loved
as I desire to love…
without consequence

Warmed by whiskey
tender rosy peaks
emerge from beneath a silk shawl,
where you are a song
in the hush of taboo,
voodoo of womanhood,
mistress of madness and passion,
a crimson caress.

II.
…the future is written upon your palm,
turn over your slender wrist…

Poets are born
sharing your peculiar Piscean moon,
they will read your words,
absorb your bravery, Anaïs.

Words which leave you
hungry, sinful, transfixed
beneath a February moon.

We will forever dream
of forbidden green apples,
sublime adornment of
kisses or stones,
love in rich hues of
(scar)let, emerald, indigo
and bask in eternal damnation
for sake of passion.

We shall dress in silk robes
painting our skin
red and unapologetic,
sway in starscapes
of your song
belly dance beneath
beautiful moonlit scars

And you will remain immortal,
a sparrow's lyrical sketch.

"Not since Anaïs Nin has the simple act of self-discovery unlocked such a steam within our female artist community. And not since I first discovered her writing on a dusty shelf in a small secondhand bookshop in an even smaller town, did that copy of *Little Birds* become the rabbit hole to my Alice-sized life. Nin's work has splendidly affected my own small life, even directed my disjointed heart in love and other delights. **Mende Smith** never could keep a house or a husband, and with three nearly grown children, she hopes the treasures of a modern writing life can be as fulfilling and vibrant as Nin's was."

Nin and Kafka Drinking Absinthe

Hollywoodland 2011

The glib of the tiny glass and the star of sugar... two drops
one draught pours, one empties

Expressing feeling is linked directly with creation.

The tell-all truth of it as plain
as the writer's wring of your hands
the cracks in the knuckles,
the paraphrased soulful being
spry as the green fairy
a living, beating record that keep's time's watch
with the taps of its fingers in nullified chambers – seeking a barren
environment where you can withdraw into it
folding your heart like a paper crane,
the morning sun caressing your wild hair
the new moon teasing the sources of all these feelings; yours and others too
its just the same old comic dueling of centuries, withdrawal

The soft chair and the pillow under...
a stack of books

There is no difference between the peasantry and the Castle

both of these views seem to have no end,
seem to offer no respite
for the drumbeat sound of typing fingers,
the scratch of the pen drawing ink
the toil of blank pages, the threat of dust
ours is the dangerous business of withering
exclamation, claims, expanses
speak for the mood to mind the gap for reason
the caricature, carve into the plot a subtle knife
the muteness of this work is defenseless in youth, interiors
the in secureness blesses every line, each biting tooth
a writer's life is inseparable, untimely as it's compensated for
a fiendish kibitzer not far from lonely,

We live in an age of progress

nearly lost to death's keynote
the long road breathes us in
ludicrous blessings impassioned, imprisoned,
we submerge
over and over the commotion comes
in waves, uncounted

Marie Lecrivain - *Venus* - 3rd century BCE (From "Cleopatra: The Search for the Last Queen of Egypt," California Museum of Science and Industry, 9/12)

Wanda VanHoy Smith spent her formative years in forests of the Pacific Northwest. Her lower education came mainly from the library and Movie House. She can't remember a time when she didn't read and dream of writing. In her teens she bought a ticket on a Greyhound bus and discovered LL Land. She met Ray Bradbury in a manuscripters club and he was her mentor for decades.

Charles Scribner's published her hard-back book for young readers which is now offered on Amazon.

In recent years her passion is poetry. Her work is in several anthologies such as *poeticdiversity*, *Valley Contemporary Poets*, *SGVPQ*, *The Night Goes on All Night*. She can be found on YouTube, in e-books and blogs such as *My Poem Rocks*, *Jerry Jazz* and *Van Gogh's Ear*. In 2013 she received an award in the Mercury Theatre L.A. County Shakespeare awards.

Hit the Road

When Ray Charles sings *Hit the Road, Jack,*
I think of Anaïs Nin and her poetry,
a young Kerouac joined the army, navy, marines
and Coast Guard all the same day.
The Navy got him before he led the
"Beat-Generation" on the way.
Given a choice the poet would have enlisted the
novel voice of Anaïs or James Joyce.
His motor ran on poetry and sex full of high
octane alcohol to the beat of a jazz drummer.
After his revelation in the service that he writes novels,
an act which he insists is perfectly normal,
Navy doctors give him an evaluation.
Military medicine men debate section 8,
believe the young poet is a psychopathic personality.
Officers conclude that Kerouac is not dangerous
but too schizoid for the navy.
They say, *Hit the Road, Jack.*
Down the road he writes a book that is
a trip that influences a free-wheeling generation
who follow Jack "On the Road."
His main character named Sal Paradise proclaims
Life is Holy every moment precious.

If I hit the road with a notebook,
write it all down as Ray Charles sings,
my main character called Sally California
reads Anaïs Nin poetry and swings.

Leeway to Live

dedicated to Anaïs Nin

An experienced Skipper who once seized life gives
her lots of advice as they are under sail in a race
on a windy day in San Francisco Bay.
He says, "Shoal draft and running with the wind
with only a head sail will give you plenty of leeway.
Don't beat upwind unless you must.
Tack in areas of the bay where wind is pleasant
and current favorable.
I have reached a time when I no longer crave
excitement or have the will to win.
Don't beat into thirty knots of wind against
troublesome currents.
Pay attention to small craft warning flags but
don't let seagull crap bombs keep you ashore.
Avoid the wear and tear of romance, deep kisses,
stormy feelings, unpredictable wind and wild sea.
Power reaches are outrageous when wind waves are
six feet high like a lover or pile of unpaid bills.
Worries can lap at your mind like tears or salt water
Give up when water splashes over the bow.
It's time to give in to doldrums and seasickness."
The old skipper hands her a bottle of rum and adds
"It's time to drop out. Tie up at the dock and fold the
spinnaker and wait for bad weather to pass."
She tosses the bottle overboard and says "Kiss my ass."
grabs the tiller with both hands and against his advice,
thinking of Anaïs, she shouts "Ready about,"
and they head back out.

Michelle Angelini - *Bee on Stacis*

Michael Tyrell's poems have appeared in many magazines, including recent editions of *The Adroit Journal, Fogged Clarity, Sycamore Review, Toronto Quarterly*, and *Verse Daily*. His collection of poems, *The Wanted*, was published by the National Poetry Review Press in 2012. He teaches writing at NYU.

The Lovers in the Lifeguard Chair

after Anaïs Nin

I'm not the first frustrated astronomer
staring farther than my corrected vision
can take me. Love not mine is better
than none. Two friends I can't save for a tryst
join me at the border where the tides
hiss, & our heckling initially makes sense,
three craning necks, what's the couple
up to, who's on top, who will break free first.
See who seems to steer the narrow bars
holding up the stalled prow good enough for borrowing.
Then it's our envy we see sharper than our pleasure—
as in the movies, we don't get to choose
the ending or topple the lovely when we want.
Like tenants emerging from a still-smoldering
building, clutching the rungs in reverse,
they come down to sand, these two—it rescues them
from falling backward; they brush off
their torn-wing garments in the capsule of light
that restores them to feature & color.
And not one of us will admit we've never done
anything that vulnerable.

Los Angeles native, **Pam Ward's** first novel, *Want Some, Get Some*, chronicles L.A. after the '92 riots. Her second novel, *Bad Girls Burn Slow*, lifts the lid off the funeral business. A UCLA graduate and California Arts Council Fellow, Pam merged writing and graphics and produced "My Life, LA: The Los Angeles Legacy Project," documenting the impact of black Angelinos on the land through poster/stories. She's published numerous L.A. poets through SHORT DRESS PRESS including the acclaimed, *Supergirls Handbook*, an anthology of black women poets from Los Angeles. www.pamwardwriter.com

Anaïs's Husband

I met Anaïs Nin's husband
dog-eared
holding an ol' bag of her
books he was donating
to the Woman's Building
where I worked.

I'd already read her work
Sex with Miller
Sex with Father
Sex with Chicks
I couldn't get enough
Her diaries, a peeled grape
gushed with the kind of carnage
my college days had yet to taste.

A self-published vixen
Nin was the queen
of the mimeo machine
running off copies
running through bodies
living end to end
with two husbands
New York & California
and enough drama,
to keep the "lie box"
tucked in her purse
bursting with ad libs.

"Did he know?"
I asked my coworker.
We watched him shuffle
down Spring Street,
one of L.A.'s filthiest
carrying that worn bag
strapped across his chest
empty now
but heavier
much heavier
since her death.

D.L. Warner is a writer and filmmaker working in Los Angeles, California. Her fiction specializes in genre erotica. To date, she was published two fantasy and four yaoi novels and released one feature film. Links to her titles and blogs can be found at http://dlwarner.blogspot.com.

Perspectives Across a Dinner Table

I give you two offerings for your entertainment pleasure.

When Ava told Ethan that he looked absolutely delicious in a tuxedo, he did not think she meant that literally. Yet there he was clutching the edge of his granite counter for dear life as his elegantly dressed companion knelt before him. Typically, Ethan enjoyed wrecking a woman's hair while she sucked his erection to bursting. However, Ava knelt with such grace then so carefully unzipped only his fly to expose his rigid erection without disturbing the 'elegant line of his tuxedo pants,' how could he dare muss even one hair that comprised that sleek French twist? It was also easier to look down and see Ava in pleasure without his hands in the way. Her expression was serenely joyful as her tongue swirled the head before she took in the shaft until her perfectly lipsticked mouth met her elegantly gloved hand. The louder he moaned, the more blissful her expression became. The suction was so powerful that it was nearly painful. Ethan erupted with a deep, throaty cry. He was left sagging against the counter while Ava gently put his flaccid member back in his pants then zipped him up.

Ava offered her gloved right hand up for Ethan to grasp and guide her to standing. She smiled at him before licking one errant, glistening drop of his completion from her plump lower lip.

"As I said, delicious," Ava laughed prettily. She picked up her neglected glass of champagne then had a swig. "And almost as good as this fine vintage. You were saying something about omelets?"

Ethan had indeed. There was even a beautiful table setting with a linen table cloth nearby for their apres theatre repast. However, he was far too much of a gentleman to accept such a gift without reciprocating. Besides, Ava wore formal attire in a way that stirred a man's hunger. He wanted to kiss her in a way that smeared her lipstick and allowed him to taste himself mingled with the champagne on her pink tongue. Perhaps, he would be permitted that indulgence if she decided to stay and allow him to unpin her hair.

Instead, Ethan firmly gasped her where the long satin corset met the floor length skirt and lifted her onto the table where he usually set up the chafing dish.

"Ethan!" Ava laughed.

"I find I'm a bit peckish for an appetizer, dear lady," Ethan murmured. "And you look delicious as well."

The skirt had a slit way up the thigh. That made exposing Ava's delights a simple matter. It was a simpler matter than Ethan imagined.

"No panties, Ava? Naughty..."

Ava giggled then sighed as Ethan flicked and sucked at the sweet nub nestled amidst soft hair. Ava was sensitive on any given day and she had been primed by a couple of glasses of fine bubbly. Still, she was a connoisseur with high standards. Fortunately, he enjoyed how she tasted and felt and responded. He had a rhythm for flicking and sucking and licking and swirling that made her slender back arch in pleasure. She even spread her thighs and lifted her hips at his tongue's entreaty to move further to the savory delights in the crease below. He jabbed his tongue there until she cried out almost harshly, demanding that he finish her. He happily obliged, adding the nip of teeth and more tugging from his lips.

"Ethan!" She cried out. Then, she sighed. Her thighs quivered and he could feel the tender, engorged nub and the wet folds beyond throbbing.

Ever the sensitive host, Ethan quickly but gently used a warm damp cloth to freshen Ava up then dabbed her dry before helping her onto her chair. After quickly washing up, Ethan poured more champagne before setting about omelet making.

"Ethan, after you dish those, would you help me unpin my hair?"

"Of course, my dear," he replied with a smile, thinking again of smearing that lipstick.

Or you could read this:

Dr. Lecter took off Krendler's runner's headband as you would remove the rubber band from a tin of caviar.

"All we ask is that you keep an open mind." Carefully, using both hands, Dr. Lecter lifted off the top of Krendler's head, put it on the salver and removed it to the sideboard. Hardly a drop of blood fell from the clean incision, the major blood vessels having been tied and the others neatly sealed under a local anesthetic, and the skull sawn around in the kitchen a half-hour before the meal.

Dr. Lecter's method in removing the top of Krendler's skull was as old as Egyptian medicine, except that he had the advantage of an autopsy saw with a cranial blade, a skull key and better anesthetics. The brain itself feels no pain.

The pinky-gray dome of Krendler's brain was visible above the truncated skull.

Standing above Krendler with an instrument resembling a tonsil spoon, Dr. Lecter removed a slice of Krendler's prefrontal lobe, then another until he had four. Krendler's eyes looked up as though he were following what was going on. Dr. Lecter placed the slices in the bowl of ice water, the water acidulated with the juice of a lemon, in order to firm them.

"Would you like to swing on a star," Krendler sang abruptly. "Carry moonbeams home in a jar."

In classic cuisine, brains are soaked and then pressed and chilled overnight to firm them. In dealing with the item absolutely fresh, the challenge is to prevent the material from simply disintegrating into a handful of lumpy gelatin.

With splendid dexterity, the doctor brought the firmed slices to a plate, dredged them lightly in seasoned flour, and then in fresh brioche crumbs.

He grated a fresh black truffle into his sauce and finished it with a squeeze of lemon juice.

Quickly he sauteed the slices until they were just brown on each side.

"Smells great!" Krendler said.

Dr. Lecter placed the browned brains on broad croutons on the warmed plates, and dressed them with the sauce and the truffle slices. A garnish of parsley and whole caper berries with their stems, and a single nasturtium blossom on watercress to achieve a little height, completed his presentation.

"How is it?" Krendler asked, once again behind the flowers and speaking immoderately loud as people with lobotomies are prone to do.

"Really excellent," Starling said. "I've never had caper berries before.

Dr. Lecter found the sheen of butter sauce on her lip intensely moving.

Hannibal – Thomas Harris Dell Publishing 2000

Only <u>one</u> of these offerings is suitable for public discourse around a water cooler.

In the 1979 preface of *Little Birds - Erotica* by Anaïs Nin, she wrote of erotica as something that was done by respectable writers only when in need of money. Erotica was something written on an empty stomach. Nin herself said that she was 'putting aside her real writing' to pursue erotica as a genre. In 2013, when all manner of genres are considered fodder for the general public and even available at big box mega-marts, writings that are overtly sexual purely for the sake of being and reveling in sexuality are still considered something unseemly that is not done by serious writers. Erotica cannot ever be literature.

I have a degree that grants me the credentials to both write and teach literature, but most of my family and few of my friends from my life back east – my formative years – talk about my writing or my accomplishments. I write primarily erotica in all manner of strange genres. Most of it has something to do with the bdsm lifestyle. I might as well be writing cookbooks on how to butcher and roast children.

And that brings me to another point. If I were writing something like that elegantly horrific scene from *Hannibal* or any of the successful torture porn films like *Saw*, I have no doubt that even my most church going family and friends would proudly talk about my accomplishments no matter how many young nubile women or occasional man I might dismember along the way. So long as I am not having them eat each other in an erotic way, my writings would be most welcome around a water cooler or at a church potluck.

Though Anaïs Nin may not have felt erotica was serious writing, she inspired me to write what I am most serious about. Erotica for me is more than putting Tab A into Slot B. It's not about exploring a weakness. Erotica is about who characters are at the most basic, human level. How they express that side of themselves chronicles how they change from the beginning of a story to the end. Despite the challenges this genre brings or how it is viewed, Anaïs Nin taught me that erotica is something that is important to study and understand, because it can never be completely repressed.

Paul Kopal - *The Four-Chambered Portrait*

Viola Weinberg served as the fi rst poet laureate of Sacramento, California. She is the author of fi ve books of poetry. As a career journalist, Weinberg worked in commercial and public radio and television and at *Mother Jones Magazine*. Her most recent poetry book is a traditionally styled Japanese book called *Enso*, a collaboration with visual artist Mario Uribe. In 2008, she was named Glenna Luschei Distinguished Poet. Currently, she is at work on *Ghosts of Electricity*, a collaboration with her husband, photographer Peter Spencer.

Paul Kopal is a self-taught life long draw-er. He was known and disliked for his artistic talent as a school boy. His drawings are spontaneous creations, automatically drawn although carefully expressed, somewhat reminiscent of aboriginal or prehistoric paintings and Picasso.

He lives in Colchester, UK. Paul is a kindred spirit in the realm of outsider art, brut, visionary, fringe, primitive, or whatever term one wishes to apply in the those (often) tiresome blanks. Regardless of what term one applies, he simply has a voice all his own.

Artist Statement: "I was born in Essex in the South East of England in 1955. I have drawn for as long as I can remember. My current way of drawing arrived fully-formed and has not yet departed. Self-taught and working intuitively, my art is a form of contemplation."

Dear Anaïs,

My clever, arching cat
You were not home
when I called, you were off
in Clichy with the degenerate
who has worn the "F" off
his typewriter as he fucks you
Forget his wretched mouth
I will exquisitely possess you with
A wandering pack of stars, roll you on
my tongue, as we create a perfect word--
I will play a Russian violin in
the verdant garden where I will bliss you
my slithery skin soft as cake frosting
then I shall kiss the hem of your wet veil--
arouse the very god in you, O, come here!
I just couldn't wait, I have arrived first
In the teeming clover, smelling of basil
carried by a summer swarm of bees from
the south, I've flown to Paris to
take you down, pluck you, taste you
my tiny, soft sparrow, run my hands
in your warm water, make you scream
like a peacock as I tumble on you
luxuriously dividing the languid day with
A raft of pearl-tipped fingers that flash
in my grip as I pin you, feed you
bite-by-bite, cupping the stem with my teeth
until it is done and the dew of us stains
our mouths and our teeth are red
as berries, lipstick everywhere
our legs twisted in a pool of silk dresses
that stinks like the sop of a vixen kit

Cindy Weinstein is a graphic designer/creative director by trade and an artist by nature. She's been writing and drawing and making things for as long as she can remember. She lives on the eastern edge of the NoHo arts district with her dog Bogart, a garden gnome, and several tame lawn flamingos. She is the founder of the Feral Fusion open mic reading and one of four current hosts. Her design business is Feral Arts LLC.

Anaïs

If you were mine
you would be mine only sometimes,
occasionally, rarely...
You see, with you I'd be like a binge drinker,
one sip and lost.
I would need to drown myself
in your thoughts,
your words,
your innocent depravity and childlike wantonness.
I would be greedy, gluttonous.
I would want to swallow you whole.
Days and nights would pass
and me, half blind,
stumbling through the mist of your vision.
Finally, responding to some primal instinct
for self preservation,
it would stop, all at once.
I'd be full,
sated, exhausted,
and I'd send you away again
to comb the cities
for more.
More exotic spices and rich flavors,
gathering stories like pollen
until you are fat with golden dust
and I am empty again.

Alicia Winski, author of *Running on Fumes* (copyright 2009 Lenore & Edgar's Publishing House), originally from Southern California, currently resides in Seattle. Winski's poetry often incorporates her love of music, ocean, and color.

Despite emerging from a family of writers, Winski dreamt instead of a singing career. A gypsy predicted a future in writing, and Alicia spent years avoiding the vocation. The prediction came true later when Winski picked up a pen after a long struggle with PTSD developed in 2002. She has yet to put her pen down. Winski has been featured in publications worldwide and is currently working on a forthcoming collection of poetry, *Naughty Girls Dream in Color*.

Beloved

dark skies pierce
crystalline
grass green orbs

butterfly soft caresses
delicately dance across
a blossoming bud

eager mouth
gentle nipping kisses
awake dormant desires

head lowers
languidly
sipping of my love

warm sinew
securing soft
sinuous femininity

a calming sea
in the eye of my
tumultuous storm

and

this

is my beloved

(originally published in *Running On Fumes* by Alicia Winski ©2009)

~Masterpiece~

Curious hands explore bristled parchment
lips licked damp, primed preparing
a silky sliding survey down, down

downy fine landscape trembling
under brush of devoted tongue flicker
flesh, salty-sweet, taut, smooth strokes

in volatile conclusion, a masterpiece
lies spent, completed, content
eyes close in triumphant delight

an artist is born this white hot night
skills acquired, inspired, honed, retired
upon the canvas of you

(originally published in *Running On Fumes* by Alicia Winski ©2009)

Fever 2012

temperature's rising, baby
sweat sleek, can't speak,
muted by desires hotter than hell

inferno blazing between quivering thighs parted,
sparked, jump started by a murmuring mouth
pressed against rigid lifts sustaining swollen tits straining
for escape into lips eager to taste the fruits of their labor

> *with skirt riding hip high, (yes)*
> *fuck me (hard) pumps capping legs spread*
> *(eagle wing wide) for you on this bed,*
> *a purring kitty's turned tiger aroused by a trainer*
> *skilled in his arts (hungry to tame her)*

> *a firm hand wielding an insistent warm whip*
> *slowly breaching a tenuous restraint forceless*
> *in holding captive a fierce, fiery feline*
> *baring talons and teeth (marking her mate)*

shake me to the core, baby, make me beg for more
singe me with your pyrotechnics, those brilliant
bright fireworks scorching starving flesh

lungs gasping, eyes pleading, hands grasping,
needing (wanting) that sweet, warm release
combustible, flammable, liquid desire
going up in flames consumed by this fire, and--

it's such a lovely way to burn
        such a lovely way to burn
            such a lovely way ...
                ... to burn*

(original Nov 2009/revision 2012 - originally published in *Running on Fumes*, copyright 2009)

Cover Photographer **Aunia Kahn** is a self-taught figurative artist, photographer, author, and curator. She combines many disciplines and invariably designs, builds, and executes characters, non-existent places, dreams, illusions, fears and fables into creation, which meld elements of classical and contemporary art. Aunia's work has constantly evolved; earlier works dealt more with her past, while her more recent creations delve into present emotional conflicts and inspirations. Her work has garnered several awards, while her national and international exhibitions and residencies range from Santa Fe, Berlin, Frankfurt, Hong Kong, Ireland, Canada, UK, New York, Los Angeles and scores in between. Aunia has curated numerous exhibitions across the country, as well as lectures at colleges and universities.

She is also the creator of the *Silver Era* Tarot deck, *Inspirations for Survivors* deck, *Lowbrow Tarot Project*, the forthcoming *Tarot Under Oath* project the author of *Obvious Remote Chaos*, and *Minding the Sea: Inviting the Muses Over for Tea*. She currently resides in Illinois with her four German Shepherds and black cat in her secret closet.

Book Designer **Jon Cunningham** is the person at Sybaritic Press what is tasked with makin' the books look all purdy like. He also writes and occasionally makes films. He has the extreme good fortune to be married to D.L. Warner.

Titles by Sybaritic Press

Demon Under Glass by *D.L. Warner*
ISBN #0971223203
$11.95

L.A. Melange: the first year of poeticdiversity
from the editors of poeticdiversity
ISBN #0971223289
$10.00

Nihilistic Foibles by *Marie Lecrivain*
ISBN #9780977867066
$10.00

A Soldier's Choice by *D.L. Warner*
ISBN #9780977867
$9.95

Stories From the Inside Edge by *Brenda Petrakos*
ISBN #09780977867073
$12.00

Naked In Paradise by *Len Richmond*
ISBN #9781604615999
$11.99

A Soldier's Fate by *D.L. Warner*
ISBN #9781606438466
$11.99

Antebellum Messiah by *Marie Lecrivain*
ISBN #9781615319659
$11.00

Ensnared Volume I by *D.L. Warner*
ISBN #9781450798303
$12.99

DemonSpawn: On The Run by *F.E. Lin, Jenny Saypaw &*
D.L. Warner
ISBN #9781607022930
$11.99

Bitchess by *Marie Lecrivain*
ISBN #9781450789455
$10.00

Alternate Lanes by *Marie Lecrivain and the staff of poeticdiversity*
ISBN #9781467546546
$9.95

Love Poems Yes...Really...Love Poems by *Marie Lecrivain*
ISBN #9781467562423
$11.99